Tea
with a
Twist

Lisa Boalt
Richardson

Photography by Lauren Rubinstein
Art Direction and Food and Prop Styling by Annette Joseph

HARVEST HOUSE PUBLISHERS
EUGENE, OREGON

Tea with a Twist

Text Copyright © 2009 by Lisa Boalt Richardson
Photography Copyright © 2009 by Lauren Rubinstein.
Photography produced/styled by Annette Joseph

Published by Harvest House Publishers
Eugene, Oregon 97402
www.harvesthousepublishers.com

ISBN 978-0-7369-2579-2

For more information about Lisa Boalt Richardson and tea, go to www.lisaknowstea.com

Original photography by Lauren Rubinstein. If you are interested in the photos in this book, you may contact Lauren at www.LARphotography.com

Design and production by Garborg Design Works, Savage, Minnesota

Printed in Hong Kong

09 10 11 12 13 14 15 / NG / 10 9 8 7 6 5 4 3 2 1

This book is dedicated to my mom,

Ruth Smelser Boalt,

a lady who loved unconditionally, listened endlessly,

and walked the talk with great faith.

Oh, how I miss having tea with you!

Contents

Introduction

The traditional English afternoon tea is such a treat, and I love to take the time to enjoy all the delights. Teatime, however, is not just limited to finger sandwiches, scones, and dainty desserts. *Tea with a Twist* was written to give the tea lover new, fun, and funky ways to spend time with friends while enjoying wonderful tea.

If you don't have fine china and your grandmother's silver, you can still enjoy a great tea party without all the fuss. The ideas are contemporary, fresh, and some are even male friendly with plenty of food! If all you have are paper plates and plastic silverware, you can still entertain and have a fabulous tea party.

Shortcuts

- If you aren't a great cook or are limited on time, make what you can and buy the rest. You could purchase some items for the party from your local bakery, market, or tea shop.
- If your budget is tight, don't feel like you need to have everything on the menu to have a great get-together. Figure out what you can afford. Even if you just serve tea and scones for a mid-morning or afternoon snack, that's fine—tea parties are for spending time with friends.
- There are so many great ready-made scones and mixes on the market now—don't be shy about trying them.
- Pick up some of the main ingredients, such as the barbeque, tandoori chicken, fajitas, or chicken salad, from your favorite local restaurant.
- The finishing touches in each chapter are just ideas. Don't feel like you have to follow all of them to have guests come over for tea.
- Presentation is not always everything. If you don't have all the accessories to make it look smashing, have a tea party anyway. Your friends will love getting together.
- You can take many shortcuts and leave some items off the menu but don't skimp on good quality tea. The tea should take center stage—after all it is called a *tea party*!
- Some ingredients listed in the recipes are marked with an asterisk (*), noting that they might not be available at your local market. Check out the resource guide at the back of the book for websites that carry those hard-to-find products.

The Basics

Hot Tea

To brew a pot of tea any size with loose leaf tea

1. Use spring water or fresh, cold water from the tap. Do not reuse water you have already boiled because the oxygen will have evaporated and this affects the taste of the tea.
2. Warm the teapot with very hot water from the tap, then discard that water.
3. Measure the tea leaves carefully into your infuser (approximately 1 teaspoon per cup of water or according to the instructions that come with your tea).
4. Heat the water until it reaches the correct temperature, generally 160 to 180 degrees for green and white tea, 190 to 200 degrees for oolong, and a full boil for black teas, herbal infusions, and fruit blends. Pour the water over the leaves immediately and cover your teapot or mug.
5. Steep the tea for the time instructed on the tea package, generally 1 to 3 minutes for green and white teas, 3 to 5 minutes for black teas and oolongs, and 5 to 10 minutes for herbal infusions and fruit blends. Over steeping can also cause the tea to taste bitter.
6. After steeping, remove the leaves.

Iced Tea

To brew one gallon of gourmet iced tea with loose leaf tea

1. Use spring water or fresh, cold water from the tap. Do not reuse water you have already boiled because the oxygen will have evaporated and this affects the taste of the tea.

2. Measure 1/3 cup tea leaves into an infuser. For teas or herbals that require a heaping teaspoon for one cup of tea like Rooibos, use 2/3 cup leaves. For this large quantity, use a large infuser so the leaves have room to expand and steep properly. You can also put the leaves directly in the teapot and strain the tea when you pour it into the gallon container.

3. Heat the water until it reaches the correct temperature, generally 160 to 180 degrees for green and white tea, 190 to 200 degrees for oolong, and a full boil for black teas, herbal infusions, and fruit blends. A six-cup teapot is a good size to use. Pour the hot water over the tea leaves immediately and cover your teapot.

4. Steep the tea for the time instructed on the tea package, generally 1 to 3 minutes for green and white teas, 3 to 5 minutes for black teas and oolongs, and 5 to 10 minutes for herbal infusions and fruit blends. Over steeping can cause the tea to taste bitter.

5. After the steeping, remove the leaves.

6. Transfer the tea to a gallon-sized pitcher and sweeten if desired. Then add enough cold tap or filtered water to make one gallon.

Basic Sweet Scones

    2 cups all-purpose flour
    1 tablespoon baking powder
    ½ teaspoon salt
    ¼ cup sugar
    ½ teaspoon vanilla
    6 tablespoons very cold butter,
        cut into small pieces
    ¾ cup heavy whipping cream

Preheat oven to 400 degrees. Place flour, baking powder, salt, and sugar in a large bowl. Cut butter into flour mixture with a pastry cutter or mixer until it looks crumbly. Add vanilla to cream and then pour into flour mixture and mix with hands until it forms a ball. Remove dough from bowl, place on a lightly floured surface, and roll out to about ½-inch thickness. Be careful not to overwork the dough or the scones will become tough. Cut with a 2-inch round cookie cutter. Place on an ungreased cookie sheet and bake for 13 to 15 minutes. Makes approximately 12. (If you decide to use a different sized cookie cutter, adjust the baking time—the larger the size, the longer they need to bake and vice versa.)

Basic Savory Scones

Follow the Basic Sweet Scone recipe except leave out the sugar and vanilla.

Flower Power
Tea Party

Do you remember the first time you ever received flowers from someone? Do you remember how special you felt? It might have been a bouquet for Valentine's Day, or maybe it was a corsage for a dance you were going to attend. Whatever the occasion, flowers just make the day a little more special.

I remember the first time someone gave me a flower. Our school was selling flowers as a fund-raiser. You could purchase a carnation and give it anonymously if you wanted to. The blooming package was delivered to the chosen person's homeroom first thing in the morning on Valentine's Day. The excitement built as the teacher called out the names of each recipient. I was one of the lucky ones. My flower went with me all day long from class to class and then home to a vase in my room. I remember I left the carnation in the vase long after it died because every time I looked at it, it reminded me of that special feeling all over again. How many of you have dried flowers from some special occasion tucked away in your house or carefully pressed in a scrapbook?

The power of a flower ignites your senses and warms your heart all at the same time. I love to walk through my local garden center and look at all the blooming plants and envision becoming a master gardener myself someday. However, the reality of my green thumb is disappointing. My goal for this season in my life is to try to keep the potted plants and flowers on my patio blooming through their growing season.

A great way to celebrate with flowers, without having to be a master gardener, is with a flower power tea party. It is a wonderful way to bring the beauty of flowers inside and make your friends feel special.

Edible flowers, grown on your back patio or on the deck of your apartment, can be used to create gourmet-looking delicacies in just a short time. If you don't possess a green thumb at all or don't have a place to grow flowers, I've listed resources in the back of this book where items can be ordered online.

The theme for this tea party is flowers, but that doesn't have to mean old-fashioned. Keep the flowers colorful and bright. It is about simple elegance with a contemporary, young, and fresh style.

Cooking with flowers may seem a bit intimidating at first, but it doesn't have to be. You may not know it, but you have probably already eaten and cooked with flowers many times. Did you know that broccoli, cauliflower, artichokes, and capers are all flowers?

The menu for this party is simple and easy to put together, but it looks like a gourmet affair that you've spent hours creating. All the recipes listed have some form of a flower as an ingredient. You can go all out with the ideas given, or you can scale back the budget and still have an unforgettable floral tea experience that you and your friends will cherish. Remember, you don't have to make it all from scratch. Make what you can, buy the rest, and decorate so it looks as though you did!

The Tea

Blooming tea* sets the stage for the big event. Blooming teas have grown in popularity since they were invented in China in the mid-1990s. A blooming tea is actually many tea leaves gathered together with a real flower or several flowers placed into the center of the leaves. It is then all hand tied together with string and wrapped in a cloth to gain its ball shape. It is unwrapped and then ready to be packaged for sale.

Preparing Blooming Teas

The beauty of the tea is not only in its flavor but also in the process that happens as you steep the tea. Place the flowering tea ball in a glass teapot and pour hot (but not quite boiling) water over it. As the tea steeps, the "flower" begins to bloom. It is a showstopper. When the leaves slowly start to open and the flower suddenly pops out of the center, your guests will be amazed. Watching this tea brew will definitely be an icebreaker and easily start off the conversation. Although the flower only opens once, the floral masterpiece may be steeped a couple more times to extract the entire flavor.

The Flowers

- For decorating purposes, the flowers do not need to be edible unless you want to stick with that theme throughout your party. Buy what is inexpensive and in the colors you love.

- The flowers for the food preparation *need to be edible flowers*. Do not eat flowers from a florist unless you know they are certified organic. You can now order some organic flower bouquets online—these may be used in foods as long as they are edible.

- Many grocery stores and gourmet markets sell edible flowers. If there aren't any stores in your area that sell them, please use the resource guide in the back of this book to find edible flowers.

- The other option for those out there with green thumbs is to grow your own. If you buy the plants from your local nursery, wait about three weeks and only cut the newly grown flowers to be sure they have not been sprayed.

- Tips for using flowers from your garden:
  - Pick your flowers in the early morning.
  - Wash the flowers gently in a salt water bath. If they are drooping a bit, perk them up by placing them in a bowl of ice water for about one minute.
  - After their bath and/or soak, carefully dry them with a paper towel and remove the petals you would like to use. The whitish part of most petals where it connects to the stem is bitter so trim that off. You may store whole flowers in a bowl of water in the refrigerator for a couple days, but it is best to use them within a few hours of picking them.

The Menu

Serves eight

Flower Power Scones
Blooming Garden Tea Sandwiches
Broccoli and Cauliflower Floret Salad
Floral-Embellished Cupcakes

Flower Power Scones

Prepare the basic sweet scones recipe according to the directions on page 9 except add ½ cup fresh edible flower petals,* such as pansies, violets, or lavender, to the butter and flour mixture. Gently mix together and continue with the recipe. Cut dough with a flower-shaped cookie cutter if desired. Serve with butter and/or lemon curd.

Blooming Garden Tea Sandwiches

Artichoke and Asiago Cheese Sandwiches

8 ounces softened cream cheese
¾ cup shredded domestic Asiago cheese
1 clove garlic, pressed
2 tablespoons basil, chopped
2 tablespoons sweet onion, finely chopped
1 14-ounce can quartered artichoke hearts,
*   drained and rinsed*
3 tablespoons sundried tomatoes packed in oil,
*   patted dry, and finely chopped*
½ teaspoon salt
⅛ teaspoon pepper
cherry tomato slices for garnish
fresh white bread

Mix all ingredients, except tomatoes and bread, together in a large bowl and refrigerate for 1 to 2 hours. Spread mixture onto fresh white bread and cut into flower shapes using a flower-shaped cookie cutter. Garnish with a thinly sliced cherry tomato in center.

Salmon Tea Sandwiches

1 8-ounce container Boursin cheese
1 tablespoon dry dill weed
8 ounces smoked salmon
fresh wheat bread
capers and fresh dill for garnish

Spread boursin cheese on bread and top with salmon. Cut out in the shape of a flower, trimming edges of salmon if necessary. Arrange capers and dill on each "flower" to look like its center—serve open faced.

Serving Suggestions

Randomly place the sandwiches on a large platter, using pickled or freshly blanched asparagus spears, pickled green beans, or pickled okra to represent the flower stems. Place small basil leaves on the "stems."

15

Broccoli and Cauliflower Floret Salad

2 heads cauliflower, cut into small florets
1 large bunch broccoli, cut into small florets

Dressing
2 teaspoons chamomile tea* or lemongrass
   chamomile tea* brewed in ⅔ cup boiling water
   for 5 minutes and cooled
2 tablespoons white wine vinegar
1 teaspoon sugar
1 tablespoon lemon
1 teaspoon lemon zest
½ teaspoon salt
¾ cup canola oil
chopped sundried tomatoes in oil and basil for garnish

Blanch cauliflower and broccoli in boiling water for
1 to 2 minutes. Drain and put in ice water to stop the
cooking. Meanwhile, whisk together the ingredients
for the dressing. Drain the cauliflower and broccoli
and put into gallon freezer bag. Pour dressing over the
vegetables and allow to marinate at least 24 hours.
To serve, put in large bowl and garnish with chopped
sundried tomatoes and basil.

Floral-Embellished Cupcakes

Prepare cupcakes using your favorite homemade cake
recipe or boxed cake mix or purchase cupcakes from
your local bakery. Embellish them by sprinkling edible
flowers* or crystallized flowers* on top of the baked
and cooled cakes or decorate the tops using a flower-
shaped stencil. Place the stencil on the top of each
cake and dust with colored fine sugar sprinkles for the
petals and poppy seeds for the center of the flower.

16

The Finishing Touches

- Sprinkle flower petals by your front door and in the foyer to draw your guests into the floral experience and entice them with what is to come.
- Use a white tablecloth to showcase the flowers. If you don't own a tablecloth, use a clean white sheet. If your budget is a little bigger, gather up the corners of the tablecloth using rubber bands and insert fresh flowers in the rubber bands. Tie a colorful wire ribbon bow around each bouquet to hide the rubber bands and stems.
- Place several already-bloomed teas in glass containers, such as bowls, goblets, large round vases, or decanters. Even a small fish bowl would do the trick. You could use one large glass container and fill it with three blooming teas, or you could use three glass containers of varying heights and put one flower in each.
- If the weather is nice and you have an outdoor area in which to eat, all of this could be moved outside.
- The flower-themed delicacies are enough to decorate the table, but if you want to go a step further, sprinkle the surface of your table with fresh petals.

- Keep the dinnerware simple and contemporary. I love all-white plates to showcase the food, but use what you have. If you feel your plates don't go with the theme at all, buy fun paper plates. A square-shaped white paper plate would be a nice contrast with all the floral shapes, but buy what you think would look best to the flowers you have chosen.
- If you use fabric napkins, try tying a colorful ribbon around each one and tucking a few small flowers under the ribbon. The ribbon and flowers make a beautiful floral napkin ring.
- If you don't have enough silverware for your crowd or want an easy cleanup, plastic cutlery is fine. If you use disposable cups, be sure that they are made for hot beverages.

Bubble
Tea Party

Bubbles have a way of setting the scene for fun. It is hard to be in a bad mood when you are blowing bubbles. A bubble floating in the air is mesmerizing to watch as it dances across the horizon. I love the way they catch the light and look iridescent in the sun as they float about.

When my kids were little, we would play and blow bubbles outside in the yard. It is one of the most inexpensive forms of entertainment, and as long as I had wind, the entertainment was there.

Making different-sized-and-shaped bubbles is easy with all the bubble accessories on the market today. Bubble machines that make bubbles automatically and continuously are available—you don't even have to worry about running out of air. As long as the bubble machine has solution in it, the entertainment is endless.

Bubbles aren't just for kids. Adults enjoy watching and making bubbles too. (In fact, when I was out shopping for a bubble machine, I found it in the wedding section of the party store, not the kid's party section.) On occasion I like to get out bubbles and blow my cares to the wind. My

dog loves to chase the soapy spheres through the yard. It is fun to watch his reaction when he catches the ball and it disappears before his very own nose.

Bubbles can be festive as well. I love wedding receptions where tiny bottles of bubbles are set at your place setting and ready to use—instead of throwing rice when the bride and groom depart. Bubbles have a way of bringing life to an occasion. At party stores you can find many kinds of bottle shapes for all different occasions.

This tea party is sure to put a smile on your face and bring out your inner child. Although some people's inner child is deeper than others, I know everyone will be certain to find it with this fun event.

The party got its Asian theme from the bubble tea country of origin, Taiwan. The food is Asian inspired with American influences. It would be a great lunch or a light summer dinner for your friends to enjoy. To enhance the bubble theme even more, everything for the party is round and in circular shapes, from the decorations to the food. I dare you not to have fun!

The Tea

The history of bubble tea doesn't date that far back. It originated in Taiwan in the early 1980s at tea stands in close proximity to schools. To compete for after-school business, the vendors began adding fruit flavors to the tea, and the kids loved it. The drinks were covered and shaken energetically to make sure the flavors infused well. This gave the tea a bubbly head and inspired the name "bubble tea."

Later tapioca pearls were added to the mixture. They looked like bubbles in the bottom, further enhancing the name. The tapioca pearls are made with sweet potato starch, cassava root, and molasses or brown sugar. Their consistency is similar to gummy bears, and they have a slightly sweet flavor. You need to serve the infusion with oversized straws to make sure you can draw the pearls from the bottom and chew them. This concoction is also known as pearl tea or boba tea.

Bubble Tea

To make bubble tea you will need:
- black lychee tea*
- large tapioca pearls*
- milk
- ice
- sweetener
- oversized straws*

You also need a cocktail shaker to mix the drink.

Prepare a pot of hot black tea according to the directions on page 7. While the tea is still hot, sweeten it with sugar or honey. Generally, you will want to use about 1 teaspoon of sweetener per cup of tea. It is better to use less sweetener than more because you can always add more later. Now chill the tea in the refrigerator. Depending on how many guests you plan on having, you may need to make several pots of tea.

Tapioca Pearls

Tapioca is very delicate, so make it right before putting the bubble tea together. In a large saucepan bring 7 cups water to a boil. Add 1 cup tapioca pearls and stir lightly so they do not stick to the bottom. Follow the cooking directions for the type of tapioca you are using. Generally, let the tapioca boil for 25 minutes and then turn off the heat. Cover and allow the tapioca to soak in the warm water for another 25 minutes. (Note: Uncooked tapioca pearls are tan—they turn black as they cook.)

Assemble the Bubble Tea

Drain the tapioca pearls and rinse them with warm water. Pour the tapioca pearls into the bottom of the cups. Pour one part tea, one part milk, and some ice into the cocktail shaker. Give it a good shake so everything gets mixed up. Pour the milk, tea, and ice over the tapioca and enjoy the drink through one of the thick straws.

Scones with Crystallized Ginger and Green Tea

Prepare the basic sweet scones recipe according to the directions on page 9 except add 1 tablespoon finely ground green tea to the flour mixture. Just before adding cream, mix in 3 tablespoons finely chopped crystallized ginger. Add cream and finish according to directions. Feel free to add more tea and/or more ginger according to taste.

Asian-O Chicken Pasta Salad

3 large boneless, skinless cooked
    chicken breasts, chopped
1 16-ounce package anelletti pasta
    (available at Trader Joe's) or any
    other round-shaped pasta
3 cups fresh blanched broccoli
1 red pepper, cut into strips
¾ cup fresh snow peas
¼ cup sliced green onion

Dressing
½ cup canola oil
½ cup red wine vinegar
4 tablespoons honey
½ teaspoon garlic powder
2 teaspoons hot sauce (optional)
1 teaspoon ground ginger
½ teaspoon salt

Whisk together all ingredients for
dressing and set aside. Cook pasta
according to package directions.
While pasta is cooking, combine
cooked, chopped chicken and
vegetables in a large bowl. Drain
pasta and add warm pasta to
chicken and vegetable mixture. Pour
whisked salad dressing over salad and
toss to combine. Cover and chill for at
least 6 hours or overnight.

Marinated Cucumber Rounds

4 large cucumbers, peeled and thinly sliced
1 small red onion, cut into small strips
seasoned rice wine vinegar
salt and pepper to taste

Combine cucumber and red onion in a large bowl. Pour enough seasoned rice wine vinegar to cover. Marinate overnight. The red onion will turn the center of the cucumber slices an iridescent color like bubbles!

Melon Ball Fruit Salad

1 large honeydew melon
1 large cantaloupe melon
½ seedless watermelon

Cut open melons and clean out seeds. Use a round scoop to carve melon into small balls. Place balls into large bowl and chill.

The Finishing Touches

- Entice your guests by placing a bubble machine near the front door to shower them with bubbles as they approach your home. This will encourage them to leave their worries behind for a while.
- Just inside the front door, place a doormat or runner made of large bubble wrap, adhered with double-stick tape, for your friends to bounce upon. Who doesn't love popping bubble wrap?
- If the weather is nice and you have space, have the party outside and move the bubble machine near the table.
- Make sure you serve everything in round bowls, platters, and plates to keep with the theme.
- Serve the tea in large clear glasses so the pearls can be seen.
- Cover your table with a tablecloth made of bubble wrap or cut out a table runner and placemats made of bubble wrap. Use the small-sized bubble wrap for placemats, runners, and tablecloth so the surface is not too uneven. Some suppliers even have bubble wrap in various colors!
- Scatter brightly colored bubble gum balls on the table or fill different sized bowls with them and use as your centerpiece. Your guests can finish the party by grabbing a few to chew on their way home or, better yet, make your grand finale a bubble blowing contest!
- Place a small bottle of bubbles at each place setting for your guests to enjoy at the party or take home.
- Hang different-sized, colorful, round paper lanterns and place a few around the table.

Tropical Tea
by the Sea Party

Some of my best memories of growing up in tropical South Florida include our family picnics at the beach. At that time, Boca Raton was a sleepy little seaside town hardly anyone had ever heard of. It would come alive for three months out of the year when all the snow birds flocked there for the winter, but the other nine months belonged to the locals. The smell of the salty ocean breeze at any seashore still takes me back to my childhood and long days spent at the beach.

To escape the heat and keep four kids entertained, my parents would load the family into the car and head for the beach, just five miles from our home. We would always go to Spanish River Park, which was adjacent to the ocean via a tunnel that went under Highway A1A. The park had playgrounds, grills, picnic tables, and huge shade trees great for climbing. It was easy to go back and forth from the park to the ocean, and we would play for hours on end.

There is just something about the salt air and the cool ocean breezes to work up an appetite. My mom would always pack a picnic lunch for the family and make her special "beach iced tea." After playing in the ocean waves and building sand castles fit for a king, I could hardly wait to sit down for our picnic and drink Mom's refreshing brew that she only made for beach outings. It was filled with fresh-squeezed orange juice from the oranges that grew right in our backyard. It was sure to quench your thirst after a hard day of playing in the water.

I never realized how blessed I was growing up with the ocean at my back door. As a teenager I virtually lived at the beach. If I wasn't in school or working, I headed to the coast for some fun in the sun. I remember riding my bike to the beach to "pre-tan" on the way there! If the weather was sunny, I knew where to find my friends on Saturday and Sunday afternoons and any day during the summer break. We had our own spot at the beach. Everyone would just show up when they could—most of the time there was at least one friend already sitting in our special place.

It is probably good that I moved away from the ocean. I can easily visualize myself becoming one of those old people whom you could mistake for your leather chair if I had stayed. I love it that much. Now when I go, I am sure to slather on the SPF 1000 instead of the baby oil I once used. I love to put my beach chair right down by the water and let the waves gently rock me as I read or sleep. The sights, sounds, and smells carry me back to simpler times and the wonderful memories of my childhood.

The sounds of the sea and sipping tea are two of my most relaxing and favorite things. If you don't live by the beach, this tea can recreate the tastes and smells of the tropics. The menu is easy to prepare and a little more adult friendly than the picnics I had as a child. Just put on your favorite beach music, rub on a little sunscreen, breathe in the tropical scents, and relax.

The Tea

Although my mom never had a recipe for her beach tea, I have tried to recreate it. It is not exact so adjust the recipe to suit your own taste buds.

Mom's Beach Iced Tea

Prepare iced tea according to directions on page 8, but don't add the cold water just yet. I like to use a good Ceylon loose leaf tea* for this recipe. Squeeze enough oranges to make 4 cups of juice. Save empty orange rinds for later use. You may substitute refrigerated fresh-squeezed orange juice (not-from-concentrate), but it is not as good as the real thing. Add orange juice to steeped tea and top off the pitcher with cold water. Sweeten to taste.

The **Menu**

Serves eight

Orange Tarragon Savory Scones
Citrus Chicken Salad
Tropical Fruit Salsa with Plantain Chips
Key Lime Coconut Bars

Citrus Chicken Salad

1½ pounds boneless, skinless chicken breasts
4 cups prepared citrus tea,* steeped double strength
1 teaspoon salt
⅔ cup light sour cream
⅓ cup light mayonnaise
6 tablespoons fresh-squeezed orange juice
  (about 1 orange)
1 tablespoon orange zest
⅔ cup celery, chopped
½ cup toasted macadamia nuts, chopped
salt and pepper to taste
8 orange rind halves and/or lettuce
orange peel to garnish

Place chicken in large sauté pan and cover with tea. Let liquid come to a boil, and then poach chicken by covering the pan and turning off the heat. Allow to poach for about 20 minutes. Chicken should be cooked all the way through. Allow chicken to rest until cool enough to handle. Combine sour cream, mayonnaise, orange juice, orange zest, celery, and macadamia nuts in a large bowl and mix well. Chop chicken and add to mixture. Add salt and pepper to taste and chill completely. To serve, slice rounded end off of a halved orange rind used to make the beach iced tea. Place a scoop of chicken salad in orange rind or serve on a bed or lettuce. Garnish with orange zest or a strip of orange peel, curled and placed on the top.

Orange Tarragon Savory Scones

Prepare the basic savory scones recipe according to the directions on page 9 except add ½ cup grated parmesan cheese, 2 tablespoons orange zest, and 1 tablespoon dried tarragon to the butter-and-flour mixture before adding cream. Finish according to directions.

Tropical Fruit Salsa with Plantain Chips

1½ cups fresh strawberries, sliced
1 cup fresh mango, diced
2 cups fresh pineapple, diced
2 tablespoons brown sugar
2 tablespoons all-fruit strawberry jam
unsweeted plantain chips

Mix the first 5 ingredients together and chill for at least an hour. Serve with plantain chips.

Key Lime Coconut Bars

Crust
1 cup butter
2 cups all-purpose flour
½ cup powdered sugar
3 teaspoons finely ground pina colada black tea*
(optional)

Bar Filling
4 eggs
2 cups sugar
7 tablespoons key lime juice
1 teaspoon coconut extract flavoring
½ teaspoon salt
1 teaspoon baking powder
4 tablespoons flour

Preheat oven to 325 degrees. Mix together pie crust ingredients in a food processor until it forms a ball. Press into a 9 x 13 pan and bake for 20 minutes. Meanwhile prepare filling by beating 4 eggs with mixer. Beat in sugar. Add lime juice and coconut flavoring and gently beat until well combined. Add salt, baking powder, and flour to mixture and gently beat until smooth. Spread filling over hot crust and bake for 25 minutes. Loosen sides and cut while still hot. Cool and sprinkle powdered sugar on top if desired. Can be refrigerated or frozen.

The Finishing Touches

- Place a sound machine by your front door and play the sound of ocean waves to greet your guests.
- If you're blessed to live by the sea or water, set your party outside.
- Use a white tablecloth, sheet, or piece of fabric to cover the table.
- Add a little extra to the table by covering the tablecloth with fish netting or fabric that looks like fish netting.
- Fill a serving tray with clean white sand and decorate with shells in various sizes. Add glass vases or bowls to the tray, fill them up with sand and shells, and add tea lights.
- Keep the feeling of the party light and airy by using soft blues and greens as accent colors.
- Light tropical-scented candles around your home.
- Use white china or paper plates.
- Decorate with tropical plants and foliage instead of flowers.
- Fill your soap dispenser in your powder room with a tropical-scented soap.
- Don't forget to play your favorite beach music softly in the background.

Mexican Fiesta
Tea Party

Fiesta simply means an event in celebration of something. The definition of a tea party to me means the same thing, so how about combining the two for the ultimate celebration?

This is not a tea party that you have to feel shy about inviting men to. The fare is hearty and plentiful. Add mariachi music to some great tea sangria, and the climate is just right for a great time. You don't even need a good reason to have a fiesta—just celebrating friends and family and life is reason enough.

The first time I traveled to Mexico, I was a senior in high school. Our small class of 13 held fund-raisers all year long to earn money to take a seven-night cruise to Mexico. We had car washes, spaghetti dinners, and yard sales to raise money for the trip.

When we stepped off the boat in Playa Del Carmen, all of the hard work paid off. The scenery was breathtaking. Although I had grown up along the ocean, the gulf beaches of Mexico weren't like anything I had ever seen before. The water was so blue and clear, and the sand was sparkling white. It was similar to a scene from a movie, walking along the cracked sidewalks and peering into small shops and primitive-looking restaurants. The smells that came from those small cafés drew you in from the streets and invited you to taste what smelled so enticing. It was there that I had my first made-from-scratch tortilla.

Our group had a great time discovering the culture of Mexico. The world of price negotiation when shopping was new to all of us. I had fun bartering and dickering over the price of the treasures I would bring home. For my mom, I purchased a beautiful hand-carved wooden vase. She loved it and kept it in a special place on her piano. It stayed right there for 20 years. When she downsized her home, she gave it back to me. It now holds a special place in my home, reminding me of my mother and that first trip to Mexico.

My Mexican culinary experience began when I was 19 and received my first waitressing job at a local Mexican restaurant called Casa Gallardo. I am not certain how authentic I looked in my uniform with my blue eyes and blonde hair, but I sure could sell the food because I loved it so much. It was there that I gained a greater appreciation of this ethnic cuisine and honed the serving skills that paid my way through college.

Mexican food is not difficult to prepare, especially now because so many great ingredients are in the local market. It has grown in popularity over the years, and Mexican restaurants are almost as commonplace as burger joints. In fact, salsa now tops ketchup as America's number one condiment. It is one of my family's favorite choices, whether we eat at home or out.

Most of these recipes have been developed through the years. Some of my ideas came from watching the chefs prepare their delicacies at the various restaurants in which I worked during my college days. Some have come from friends who knew how to entertain fiesta style. The preparation is not labor intensive and the ingredients are simple.

Whether you have a great reason to celebrate or you just feel like having a party, you won't be disappointed when you pull out the salsa, mix up a batch of tea sangria, and invite some friends over for a Mexican fiesta-style tea party.

The Tea

It's so good, you will probably need to make several gallons for the party!

Tea Sangria

Ceylon tea*
3 oranges, ends cut off and sliced (If you can find blood oranges, use them)
3 limes, ends cut off and sliced
2 cups pomegranate juice cocktail
½ cup sugar
orange and lime slices to garnish glasses

Prepare one gallon iced tea according to directions on page 8 except when finished steeping, don't immediately add water. Remove leaves and pour into a heat-resistant one-gallon container. Stir in sugar until it dissolves. Add pomegranate juice and sliced fruit. Fill the container with water up to top and chill well. To serve, pour tea from a pitcher into glasses filled with ice. Garnish with orange or lime slices.

Jack Cheese and Green Chili Scones
Chips and Salsa
Bean Dip with Scoop-style Chips
Steak Fajita Salad with Zesty Lime Vinaigrette
"Faux" Fried Ice Cream Topping

Chips and Salsa

Choose your favorite tortilla chips and salsa

Bean Dip with Scoop-style Chips

1 8-ounce package cream cheese, softened
2 16-ounce cans refried beans
1½ teaspoons cumin
1½ teaspoons garlic powder
½ teaspoon onion powder
1 teaspoon oregano
1½ teaspoons chili powder (add a bit more
*   if you like it hot)*
½ teaspoon paprika
2 cups jalapeno jack cheese, shredded
1 small can sliced black olives, drained
Scoop-style tortilla chips

Preheat oven to 350 degrees. Mix first 8 ingredients together and blend until smooth. Place bean mixture into a greased 9 x 13 pan. Scatter cheese over top of mixture and sprinkle olives on top. Bake 20 to 30 minutes or until heated through and cheese is melted. Serve with scoop-style tortilla chips.

Jack Cheese and Green Chili Scones

Prepare the basic savory scones recipe according to the directions on page 9 except add one cup shredded jalapeno jack cheese and 1 4-ounce can drained and dried diced green chili peppers to the butter and flour mixture. Stir until blended, add cream, and finish the recipe.

Steak Fajita Salad with Zesty Lime Vinaigrette

3 pounds top sirloin steak

Marinade
2 oranges, juice and zest
2 limes, juice and zest
1 cup cilantro, chopped
1 cup onion, finely chopped
4 tablespoons olive oil
2 teaspoons salt
1 teaspoon pepper

Combine all ingredients together in a gallon-size freezer bag. Place steak in bag with marinade and let marinate 4 hours. Remove steak from marinade and grill steak on hot grill approximately 5 minutes on each side or until medium rare. Take off grill and let rest for 15 minutes.

Zesty Lime Vinaigrette
4 limes, juice and zest
1 cup olive oil
4 teaspoons sugar
1 tablespoon salt
½ teaspoon pepper

Combine all ingredients in a jar and shake well.

Salad
2 10-ounce bags prewashed romaine lettuce
2 red bell peppers, cut into thin strips
1 cup cilantro, chopped
2 cups cherry or grape tomatoes

In a large bowl, put all the salad ingredients together. Cut steak in thin slices and place on platter. Put the salad dressing in a bowl next to the salad and allow your guests to spoon out dressing over the salad and meat.

"Faux" Fried Ice Cream Topping

Here is a great way to get the flavor of fried ice cream without having to fry it!

4 cups cornflakes, coarsely crushed
½ cup butter
½ cup brown sugar
¼ teaspoon cinnamon
¼ teaspoon salt
½ gallon of your favorite vanilla ice cream

Preheat oven to 400 degrees. Place crushed cornflakes on a parchment paper-lined cookie sheet that has sides. Put butter and brown sugar in a small saucepan and melt together. Allow it to come to a boil and continue boiling for 3 minutes, stirring constantly. Remove from heat and stir in cinnamon and salt. Pour hot mixture over cornflakes and bake for 3 to 6 minutes or until brown. Allow to cool and then break into large chunks. May be stored in an airtight container. To serve, scoop vanilla ice cream into bowls and top with a generous portion of the cornflake mixture.

The Finishing Touches

- Use ponchos or Mexican blankets to cover tables.
- Buy a few Mexican tiles from a home supply store and use them as a runner on top of the poncho or blanket. The tiles could also be used as placements at each individual setting.
- Decorate the table with natural items such as limes, oranges, chili peppers, bell peppers, tomatillos, and tomatoes. Place them in large glass vases or flat ceramic bowls. Spread them across the table and on top of the tiles if you don't want to use containers.
- Buy a few small cacti in clay pots and place them among the fruit and vegetables to add to the centerpiece.
- Use vibrant colors to decorate your table and surroundings.
- Play mariachi music in the background.
- If you have enough in the budget, serve the sangria in Mexican bubble glassware.
- If the party is at night, place tea lights in Mexican glasses and/or vibrantly colored candles in chunky wooden or wrought iron candlestick holders.

Southern Tailgate
Tea Party

Something happens in the fall in the South long before we see the leaves changing color or feel the briskness in the air. It is the beginning of football season. Friday nights are filled with high school football games and the sounds of marching bands. On Saturdays devoted college football fans fill enormous stadiums to the brim—each fan decked out from head to toe in the colors of their team.

Along with all this excitement comes the art of tailgating. It truly has become an art form, and in some families and circles of friends, it is a prerequisite to the football game. Some would even go so far as to have a tailgate party whether or not they plan to watch the game live or on television.

There are tailgating associations, trade shows, websites, forums, and blogs for the diehard. Did you know that there is actually a "commissioner of tailgating"? His name is Joe Cahn, a Southerner from Louisiana. He contends that tailgating unites people

better than any other alfresco event. With that idea in mind, a Southern tailgate tea seems like a great way to celebrate food, family, friends, and football!

I must confess that I am not a Southerner by birth. Although most of my childhood was spent in South Florida, I have been told that doesn't make me Southern. Most of my college days were spent in Southern California, and *that* is most definitely not the "South."

I am Southern by marriage and also by choice. I am married to a man from Louisiana, and I have lived in the true South most of my adult life. I have come to call this place my home, and I love and appreciate the people, climate, and scenery that make up this unique part of the country. I even seem to have acquired a Southern accent along the way. Because my parents are from Ohio, every now and again my "Yankee" accent surfaces— my children are quick to point out that it is very wrong. My husband likes to tell me I can teach our children manners, but he'll teach them how to talk!

Confessions aside, I was in my mid-twenties the first time I ever tasted Southern sweet tea. It was June, and I had just moved from Southern California to North Carolina. My body's ability to withstand the heat and humidity was a distant memory. Hot and tired from moving, I looked for some relief at a fast food drive-through. I ordered an iced tea and proceeded to add a dab of artificial sweetener, as was my custom at the time. With my first sip, I just about gagged! It had arrived already sweetened way beyond my liking—the sweetener I added had made the situation even worse. It was then that I discovered that if you order tea in the South without specifying which type, you will get not only sweet tea but exceedingly sweet tea!

Southerners drink iced tea all year round. When football starts below the Mason-Dixon line, it still feels like summer. Toward the end of the season, however, you will be wrapped up in blankets, wearing gloves, and wondering if your toes will ever be warm again. This tailgate tea party lists two types of tea. The first is iced for the early tailgating parties or for those that never venture beyond iced. The second is hot for those who have stuck it out all season long and are cold to the bone. Regardless of which type of tea you might enjoy, this teetotal feast is all Southern and can be enjoyed even if you aren't blessed to live in the South.

The Tea

Iced tea is known as the "table wine of the South." It is a staple in most homes. If you have any manners at all, you always offer your guests a glass of the iced beverage no matter how short the visit. My Yankee upbringing, as my husband likes to call it, has influenced how sweet I make my tea. My mom always made unsweetened iced tea when I was growing up, and I now like it somewhere between the Yankee and Southern style when it comes to sweetness. Whichever way you like it, be sure to start with a good quality loose leaf tea. For those of you who long for something hot to drink when the temperature drops later in the season, brew up some hot tea. Some diehards might call you wimpy and then ask for some themselves.

I am not sure how many southern states claim to be the peach state, but I live in Georgia, and we are the only ones that put it on our license plates! Regardless of which state produces the most of this delectable fruit, the flavor makes a great tea.* I also think a ginger peach tea* is very nice. Both are great iced and hot and pair well with the menu. Prepare iced or hot tea according to the directions on pages 7 and 8.

The Menu

Serves 12-15

Sweet Potato Pecan Scones
Kick-off Pimento Cheese Dip with Crudités
Cheesy Cornbread Sausage Balls
Smokey Tea First Down Barbeque
Touchdown Tea Infused Pecan Brittle

Sweet Potato Pecan Scones

You will probably need to double this recipe to allow for seconds! Prepare the basic sweet scones recipe according to the directions on page 9 except replace white sugar with brown sugar. And after cutting the butter into the flour mixture, add in 1 teaspoon cinnamon, ½ cup roasted, finely chopped pecans, and ½ cup canned sweet potatoes or yams. Be sure to mash the sweet potatoes well and stir to gently combine. Add only ¼ cup of cream and form into a ball. If too dry, add a little more cream. Finish the recipe as directed. Serve with sweet potato butter.*

Kick-off Pimento Cheese Dip with Crudités

1 pound extra sharp cheddar cheese
    (do not use pre-shredded)
8 ounces cream cheese, softened
⅛ cup mayonnaise
1 4-ounce jar diced pimentos, drained
    (roasted red peppers)
¼ teaspoon onion powder
Dash of hot sauce
¼ cup chopped jalapenos, optional (if you like it a bit hot)
crudités for dipping

Combine all ingredients in a large bowl and mix well. Chill. Serve with crudités such as carrots, celery, and cherry tomatoes.

Cheesy Cornbread Sausage Balls

1 1-pound package breakfast sausage
1½ cups self-rising cornmeal mix
1¼ cups freshly grated sharp cheddar cheese
    (do not use pre-grated)
1 4-ounce jar pimentos, drained and chopped
¼ cup canned jalapenos, chopped
dash of hot sauce

Preheat oven to 400 degrees. With your hands, mix all the ingredients in a large bowl until well blended. Use a 1½ inch scoop and form balls. Place balls on ungreased baking sheet that has sides and bake for 15 to 18 minutes or until lightly brown. Sausage balls may be frozen uncooked or cooked.

Smokey Tea First Down Barbeque

1 3-pound boneless beef chuck roast
1 medium onion, chopped
½ cup celery
14 teaspoons Lapsang Souchong tea, divided*
1½ cups ketchup
1 cup light brown sugar, packed
¼ cup vinegar
1 tablespoon dry mustard
2 teaspoons salt
½ teaspoon chili powder
1 teaspoon paprika
½ teaspoon garlic powder
prepared coleslaw

Steep 10 teaspoons tea in 6 to 7 cups hot (freshly boiled) water for 4 minutes, and then remove the tea leaves. Place beef roast, chopped onion, and celery in a large pot. Cover with tea. Bring to a boil and then reduce heat. Cover and simmer for 2½ to 3 hours or until meat is tender. Remove from liquid and strain, saving vegetables. Allow to cool, and then shred beef.

Sauce

Steep remaining 4 teaspoons of tea in 2 cups boiling water for 4 minutes. Combine one cup tea, ketchup, brown sugar, vinegar, mashed and strained vegetables from beef, and rest of seasonings in a large saucepan. Cover and simmer for about 1 hour, stirring occasionally. If mixture becomes too thick, add remaining tea. Add shredded beef to sauce and stir until combined. May be served with or without buns. To be really Southern, top with coleslaw!

Touchdown Tea Infused Pecan Brittle

You might want to make extra, but make it one batch at a time or it won't work in the microwave.

½ cup light corn syrup
1 cup sugar
1½ cups pecans, coarsely chopped
½ teaspoon salt
1½ teaspoons cinnamon black tea,* finely ground
1 tablespoon butter
1 teaspoon vanilla
1 teaspoon baking soda

Combine light corn syrup and sugar in a large, microwave-safe glass bowl. Stir until combined and microwave for 3 minutes. Stir in pecans and salt and microwave 3 minutes. Stir in tea and butter and microwave 1 minute. Stir in vanilla and baking soda. Combine well and pour onto a parchment paper-lined cookie sheet. Quickly spread mixture into a thin layer and allow to cool. Break into small pieces.

The Finishing Touches

- Whether you do this picnic style or in the back of your vehicle, the decorations for the party should be simple. The focus should be on your team, the colors that represent them, and on the great fare.

- For tablecloths find some fabric and effortlessly cover your table or tailgate. If lucky enough to find one with your team logo on it, use that. You can also use stadium blankets or an inexpensive, washable, woven or braided cotton rug as a tablecloth or tailgate cover.

- I love the idea of sturdy paper plates for this party because when the eating is over, the game begins, and you don't want to worry about cleanup for this meal.

- You can use large paper napkins or reasonably priced dishtowels or washcloths as napkins. Have an ample supply on hand because barbeque is messy. When shopping, keep your team in mind and shop for things with the team colors.

- Wet naps are good to have on hand too.

- Serve your side dishes and utensils in baskets lined with colorful napkins. Tie team-colored ribbons to the basket handles or around the basket edges.

- When making your tea hot, keep it in a thermos or insulated pitcher. Make more than you think you need because as the temperature drops, you'll want something to warm you up. You can always use the leftovers to make iced tea when you get home.

- When making your tea cold, have plenty of ice on hand. Some of the football weekends can be as hot as an SEC (southeastern conference) rivalry.

All About Chocolate
Tea Party

My membership into chocoholics anonymous started at a very young age. As far back as I can remember, chocolate has always been my dessert of choice. Based on the stories that have been passed down, I think that I inherited my love of chocolate from my mother's side of the family.

I was told that my grandmother craved Hershey's bars when she was pregnant with my mother. She must have eaten quite a few because my mom's nickname when she was born was "Hershey baby." My grandfather also had quite an affinity for chocolate. He was a plump old man, and my grandma always had him on a diet.

However, he kept a private stash of tempting chocolate morsels out in the trunk of his car. We could never figure out how he kept them from melting. When Grandpa said he needed some air, we knew what he really needed was a chocolate fix! He would then sneak outside and eat a bit of velvety sweet goodness. We teased him until the day he died about his sinful hidden temptations.

My father, although not a confirmed chocoholic, played a large role in helping me discover chocolate as an epicurean delight. When I was young, he and I would go on dinner dates. My father felt it was important for his daughters to know proper table etiquette as well as how a young man should treat a lady on a date. From opening my car door to pulling my chair out at the dining table, my dad gave me a great example of what I should expect from a boy who wanted to date me.

One of our favorite places to go was a restaurant named Pal's Captain's Table near my hometown of Boca Raton, Florida. Although we weren't wealthy, my dad would tip the maitre d' to secure a table with a view of the Intracoastal Waterway. I felt like a princess as he pulled out my chair to what I thought was the best seat in the house. As we sat and watched the boats and yachts go by and ate, my dad and I would talk about how to be a lady and use proper table manners.

While I learned dining etiquette and loved spending time with my dad, the dessert cart was the most memorable part of our outings. A man dressed in a formal tuxedo would present the most tantalizing sweets. Though I knew which one I wanted from the very beginning, we would patiently listen as he described in detail all the choices on the trays. When he finished with his dessert dissertation, I would always order the chocolate cake. But this was not just any old chocolate cake. It seemed to be a mile high and filled with the richest, densest chocolate filling I had ever tasted. I would savor the cake and let it melt in my mouth as I watched the seagulls and the boats pass by. I was hooked!

The slice of rich decadence was so large that there was always some to take home. I would savor the flavor for a few days afterward and look forward to the next time Daddy and I could go to dinner again. I don't recall what I ordered for the main course, but I will never forget my desserts!

As I grew older, my father once again introduced me to the ever-expanding wonders of chocolate. I thought I was doing fine eating my convenience store candy bars until he introduced me to gourmet chocolate. At 16, my dad took me on a special father-daughter shopping trip. We mainly window-shopped and dreamed, but there was one purchase that changed my taste buds forever. My father wanted to buy something special and sweet for me to take home and remember our day, but no ordinary chocolate would do. This was Godiva! He bought a one-pound box of dark and milk chocolate medallions. I had never tasted anything so good, and my palate now knew the difference. Although I hate to call myself a chocolate snob, I think I have become one.

Chocoholics around the world must have jumped for joy a few years back when research concluded that chocolate is actually good for us. Some might have suspected it all along, but now we have proof. Chocolate has properties that lift your spirits, but in addition to that, it is filled with antioxidants that benefit your body. Tea is loaded with these wholesome antioxidants as well. Putting the two together is truly a nutritious pleasure not to be missed.

Now that you know it is good for your heart and mind, why not pamper yourself and your friends with a tea and chocolate epicurean experience? I am always on the lookout for the next best chocolate delight, and I believe this tea party has fulfilled my search! It is all about chocolate from your first sip to your last bite.

The Tea

Choose a good quality loose leaf tea for the party and prepare the hot tea according to the directions on page 7. The one I like is called "chocolate truffle"*—it is milk chocolaty and has chocolate bits in it. Be prepared to make several pots of "hot chocolate tea" because your guests will love drinking their chocolate without all the calories!

Triple Chocolate Scones
Chocolate Strawberry Salad
Chocolate Tea and Spice-encrusted Wild Salmon
with White Chocolate Green Tea Sauce
Easy Microwave Bittersweet Chocolate Truffles

Chocolate Strawberry Salad

2 cups strawberries, sliced and hulled
2 10-ounce bags prewashed red leaf lettuce
½ small red onion, sliced thinly
2 tablespoons plain or chocolate covered roasted
    cacao nibs*

Dressing
4 tablespoons raspberry jam
4 tablespoons raspberry vinegar
2 tablespoons honey
4 teaspoons canola oil

Whisk together all the dressing ingredients in a small bowl. Combine strawberries, lettuce, and red onion in large bowl. Pour dressing over salad and toss. Sprinkle the cacao nibs over top and serve.

Triple Chocolate Scones

Prepare the basic sweet scones recipe according to the directions on page 9 except add ¼ cup each of white chocolate chips, bittersweet chocolate chips, and semisweet chocolate chips to the mixture before rolling out dough. Serve with strawberry preserves or lemon curd.

Chocolate Tea and Spice-encrusted Wild Salmon with White Chocolate Green Tea Sauce

Spice Rub

2 tablespoons cumin
2 tablespoons chili powder
1 tablespoon ground coriander
1 tablespoon salt
1 tablespoon pepper
1½ teaspoons cinnamon
1½ teaspoons brown sugar
1½ teaspoons red pepper flakes
2 teaspoons finely ground chocolate black tea*

Combine all the spices together in a small bowl until well mixed.

White Chocolate Green Tea Sauce

6 tablespoons butter
6 teaspoons all-purpose flour
2 cups prepared lemon green tea or vegetable broth
　　(may also use plain green tea)*
4 tablespoons fresh lemon juice
4 ounces white chocolate
¼ teaspoon salt
dash of nutmeg
4 pounds wild fresh salmon

Dry salmon well and rub spice mixture all over. Set salmon aside. Melt butter in a medium saucepan over medium heat. Whisk in flour and blend. Add green tea or broth. Let the sauce simmer over low heat for about 15 minutes or until slightly thickened. Add lemon juice, white chocolate, salt, and nutmeg and stir until chocolate is melted. Keep warm. Bake, broil, or grill salmon until done. Put fish on a large platter. Pour chocolate sauce in a small pitcher or gravy boat and serve.

Easy Microwave Bittersweet Chocolate Truffles

½ cup heavy cream
3 tablespoons butter, cut into chunks
2 tablespoons sugar
1 tablespoon vanilla
10 ounces good quality bittersweet chocolate
    (60%); I like to use Ghirardelli bittersweet
    chocolate chips.* If not using chips, break
    chocolate into small pieces.
½ teaspoon salt

Cocoa Mixture

Mix ⅓ cup unsweetened cocoa and ⅓ cup powdered sugar together. For a saltier taste, add ⅛ teaspoon salt.

Microwave cream, butter, and sugar in a 2-quart microwavable glass bowl on high for 1½ minutes. Stir well. Heat an additional 1 minute longer or until mixture comes to full boil. Stir vanilla and chocolate into cream mixture until chocolate is completely melted. Add salt and blend. Chill until firm enough to shape into balls—about 3 hours. Shape into 1-inch balls and, if desired, roll in cocoa mixture. Store in covered container in refrigerator. Makes about 2 dozen.

The Finishing Touches

- This party would be great to set up as an interactive cooking party for girlfriends or couples if your kitchen can accommodate the crowd. You can even use the table for some stations.

- Make the truffles three hours ahead of time so they will be ready to be shaped.

- Set up cooking stations and pair up your guests. Lay out all the ingredients, recipes, and supplies for your guests to start cooking. Have two people work on the salad, two work on the salmon, two work on the scones, and two people shape truffles.

- Keep your table setting simple and let the food be the focus.

- If you would like a centerpiece, fill up three glass bowls or vases with different kinds of chocolate chips—one for milk chocolate, one for white chocolate, and one for semisweet or bittersweet chocolate.

- This tea party would also make a wonderful and romantic couples party. Place a bouquet of red roses and some loose petals on the table.

- Prepare the truffles ahead of time, place them in small decorative boxes, and set one box at each place setting as a party favor.

- Give your guests an extra treat and fill up your powder room soap dispenser with chocolate-scented soap.

Indian Chai
High Tea

Chai tea, as most Americans know it, is a spiced tea originating from India. "Chai" simply means "tea." The chai tea we know in America is actually called "masala chai" for the ingredients that are added to give it its unique taste. Masala is a mixture usually comprised of cardamom, cinnamon, ginger, cloves, and black pepper. This masala mixture is not only used in tea but in many Indian dishes as well.

Indian food is somewhat of a new adventure for me. As I began to study tea and learn about the different cultures that surround the beverage, I found that Indian teas were on my preferred list. I was then lured into trying Indian food. The flavorful food is so unique and can be a bit spicy, just the way I like it. In fact, I have grown to love it. Having a cup of masala chai, made the traditional way, after your Indian feast is a great way to end your meal.

India is one of the largest producers of black teas in the world. They are also a huge consumer of their own crop. However, their tea traditions do not date back that far. It wasn't until they came under British occupancy in the nineteenth century that tea was cultivated. Although

there are places in India, especially in the finer hotels, that serve tea in the "English afternoon tea" style, most Indians do not take tea in that manner in their daily lives. Teatime to the common Indian is anytime and all the time.

While studying Indian teas, I found that the way Indians serve tea is very interesting. *Chai wallahs* are young boys who are tea vendors. They sell tea on the street corners and in the train stations all across India. They are quite ambitious and can be heard shouting *"chai"* or *"chai-ya"* across the city streets and in the stations. They have makeshift kitchens with kettles and brass pots brewing a mixture of tea with spices, warmed milk, and sugar throughout the day.

The Indian version of a disposable cup is called a *kullarh*. It is a primitive earthenware cup made of native clay. Once the tea is finished and the cup is empty, the pottery is tossed alongside the road or out of the train window—broken *kullarhs* are scattered all along the sides of Indian streets.

Spiced masala chai could be compared to a mulled spiced cider or wine in America. The aroma from the tea alone is so inviting on a cold winter's day. The inspiration for this get-together comes from the tea itself—the spices used in the infusion inspire this fireside party.

By following the true definition of a high tea (a meal with tea served as a supper in the evening), this tea party is a hearty meal your guests, both male and female, will warm up to very quickly. The food is Indian inspired, and most of the ingredients can be found easily at your local market. If you have access to an Indian market, you may get motivated to make your own recipes.

The Tea

There are many instant chai tea blends on the market today, but I don't recommend them. Many instant teas do not have the best flavor, and they often contain unnatural or unnecessary ingredients to the mix. Making spiced chai is not hard to do so, don't be afraid to try. You can be adventurous and come up with your own concoction or buy a good quality loose leaf spicy masala chai.* There are several ways to steep this exotic blend, but I prefer the following method.

Traditional Chai Tea

1. Place 7 to 9 tablespoons of loose leaf chai blend tea in a large size saucepan. Add 4½ cups of water and 3 cups of milk to the pan. Stir constantly and bring to a boil.

2. Reduce the heat and let it simmer for 3 to 5 minutes. Remove from heat and stir in 2 to 3 tablespoons of sugar or honey.

3. Strain the mixture with a sieve, pour into a pot, and serve.

I like using vanilla soy milk in mine. I think the thickness and flavor of the milk add to the tea's tasty brew.

The Menu

Serves eight

Masala Chai Scones
Tandoori Roasted Chicken Thighs
Curried Cauliflower
Nan Bread or Pita Bread purchased ready made
Coconut Pistachio Cookies

Masala Chai Scones

Prepare the basic sweet scones recipe according
to the directions on page 9 except add 1 tablespoon
finely ground, spicy masala chai* to the butter and
flour mixture and stir in well. Add the cream and finish
the recipe.

Tandoori Roasted Chicken Thighs

If you have stone roasting pans, use them—they hold the heat similar to a tandoori oven.

4 pounds boneless, skinless chicken thighs
2½ cups plain yogurt
1 medium onion, chopped
6 garlic cloves
2 tablespoons fresh ginger, minced
2 tablespoons masala chai tea,* finely ground
1 teaspoon cumin
1½ teaspoons turmeric
2 teaspoons cayenne pepper
1 teaspoon paprika
2 teaspoons salt
1 medium onion, thinly sliced
chopped cilantro for garnish

Combine the yogurt and the remaining ingredients in a large bowl. Mix well. Cut several slits in each piece of chicken with a sharp knife. Add the chicken to the yogurt mixture and coat well. Cover and marinate at least 8 hours, or better yet overnight.

Heat oven to 500 degrees. Place chicken in roasting pans (you will probably need 2) and cook for 15 minutes or grill the chicken for about 7 minutes on each side or until juices run clear. Place chicken on large platter and sprinkle chopped cilantro and onions over the top. Serve with chutney.

Curried Cauliflower

2 large heads of cauliflower
3 tablespoons butter
2 tablespoons canola oil
1 teaspoon salt
1 teaspoon curry powder (more if you like it spicy)
Cilantro for garnish

Cut cauliflower into small pieces, place in a steamer, and steam approximately 4 minutes. Heat butter and oil in a large frying pan until melted. Add cauliflower and stir-fry until cauliflower is cooked through but still slightly crunchy. When almost done, sprinkle salt and curry powder over cauliflower and stir until blended well. Garnish with cilantro sprigs.

Coconut Pistachio Cookies

¾ cup butter, softened
¾ cup sugar
1 large egg
1½ teaspoons vanilla
½ teaspoon salt
2¼ cups all-purpose flour
1 cup coconut
½ cup pistachios, finely chopped
whole pistachios for tops of cookies

Preheat oven to 350 degrees. Beat butter on medium speed, and then gradually add sugar. Add egg and vanilla and mix well. Combine flour and salt and slowly add to butter mixture. Stir in coconut and pistachios until well blended. Use a small scoop and form dough into 1-inch balls. Place on cookie sheet and flatten. Put one whole pistachio in the center of cookie and press in slightly. Bake for 12 to 15 minutes or until set. Don't overcook or allow tops to brown. Cool on cooling rack. Dough or baked cookies may be frozen.

The Finishing Touches

- Use warm colors to decorate for the tea: reds, oranges, and golden yellows.
- Place chunky, carved dark wooden or brass candlesticks on the table with cream or gold candles.
- Use Indian linens, a sari, or a pashmina as a tablecloth or table scarf.
- Scatter bangle bracelets across the table.
- For a personal touch, make napkin rings/place cards with bangle bracelets by writing your guests' names on place cards, cutting a hole in one corner of each card, and embellishing the cards with plastic jewels. Next, tie the place card to a bangle bracelet and slip a napkin through the bangle.
- Use a dark wooden tray as a tea tray.
- Fill up small rustic clay pots or wooden bowls with cardamom, cinnamon sticks, and cloves mixed with dried lentils.
- Have a bowl of pistachios for your guests to snack on while preparing last-minute items.
- Make a floral garland out of marigolds and chrysanthemums and drape it across your table. To create the garland, remove the stems of all flowers, thread an embroidery needle with heavy-gauge or embroidery thread, and sew the flowers together by stitching through the thickest part of each flower head.
- Serve your last pot of tea and plate of cookies fireside if possible.
- Toss Indian inspired floor pillows on the floor near the fire for your guests to sit or lean on.

Under–the–Table
Tea Party

When you were a child, do you remember making tents inside your house with old sheets and blankets? My siblings and I would spend hours with our friends making the most elaborate tents, covering the entire family room. It was so fun to crawl around inside your creative work! It was even better if we were allowed to eat inside the tents as if we were really camping.

A wonderful lady named Linda Allen, who has become a second mom to me, gave me a great idea when I was a new mom. That idea has become the inspiration for this tea party. She suggested that I have an eat-under-the-table day with my son. It is similar to eating under the tent without the mess of the blankets.

The ritual started one rainy day with my very active three-year-old son named Zach. I just dreaded rainy days when he couldn't go outside and use up some of his energy. We needed something fun to do inside. I can still see Zach's look of excitement when I told him we were going to eat under the table. He had never been so helpful when setting "the table" before. He quickly helped me get out placemats and paper plates. We

placed a tablecloth over the table and crawled under it. As I hunched over and ate my PB and J sandwich with my son, I knew this would not be the last time we would do this.

What started out as a desperate act to amuse my son on a rainy day became a tradition. Once I had my daughter, Kate, Zach was anxious for her to grow old enough to share in our adventure. Sometimes we would share our secret lunch style with their friends. I am sure they thought Mrs. Richardson was crazy. Come to think of it, I think my children's friends still think I am crazy. My daughter likes to reassure me that it is crazy in a good way, though.

Although my children would have loved to eat under the table every day, I saved it for special occasions. I have to admit that I sometimes used it as a bribe for good behavior or to get them to do some of their chores. Whatever the reason, the reaction was always the same—excitement. Children think it's wonderful when adults condone breaking table etiquette every once in a while. We are always telling our kids to chew with their mouths closed and use their napkins not their shirts, and of course there is a time and place for proper manners, but when you are under the table, you can forget about a few of them.

This tea party is about breaking the rules and having fun. Kids will love to do this. It doesn't have to be a formal affair, and you should keep it simple. Although this party is planned for young ones, you just have to be a kid at heart to participate. The only catch is that if you sit under the table, you have to be able to stand back up!

The Tea

Children love fruity teas. If you have concerns about caffeine, try a blend of dried fruits and herbs.* If caffeine is not an issue, there are many fruity loose leaf teas on the market that would suffice. I think kids like the idea of drinking hot tea but don't like to drink it very hot. Prepare a pot of hot tea according to the directions on page 7 ahead of time, presweeten it while it is hot so the sugar dissolves, and let it cool a bit before you serve it to the children. This will also help keep the kids from adding too much sugar to the tea—I have witnessed many heaping spoonfuls of sugar going into just one cup.

The Menu
Serves approximately eight

PB & J Sconewiches
Rolled Ham Horns
Cheese Critters
Toothpick Fruit Caterpillars
Crispy Wormy Mud Balls

P B & J Sconewiches

Prepare the basic sweet scones recipe according to the directions on page 9 except mix in ½ cup peanut butter chips to the butter and flour mixture. Then add cream and finish according to directions. Let cool. To serve, cut each scone in half and spread your child's favorite jelly in the middle. Serve as a sandwich...a sconewich!

Rolled Ham Horns

Buy your favorite deli ham and roll up. Make sure to have the kids "blow their horns" before they eat them.

Cheese Critters

1 package of your favorite cheese, cubed and allowed to warm to room temperature (mozzarella is the easiest to work with)
1 package pretzel sticks

Place a pretzel stick through 3 cheese cubes. Make as many critters as you think your crowd will eat or let the kids make them.

Toothpick Fruit Caterpillars

toothpicks
green and red grapes, washed

Poke a toothpick through 3 grapes to resemble a caterpillar. You can alternate colors on each toothpick or use all one color on each toothpick. Be creative!

Crispy Wormy Mud Balls

3 tablespoons butter
1 package (approximately 10 ounces) or 4 cups small marshmallows
6 cups crisp rice cereal
2 cups crushed Oreos
gummy worms, cut in half
cooking spray
wax paper or parchment paper

Melt butter in large saucepan. Add marshmallows and stir until melted completely. Remove from heat and stir in crisp rice cereal until well blended. Let cool slightly. Coat hands in cooking spray to keep mixture from sticking to hands and scoop up a small handful. Place gummy worm in center of scoop and roll into a ball, hiding the worm in the center of the ball. Roll in crushed Oreos, pressing the cookie crumbs onto each ball, and place on waxed paper or parchment paper. Cool completely.

The Finishing Touches

- Placing an inexpensive plastic tablecloth under the table is a good idea.
- If you have the space and the weather is nice, have the party under a patio table (a good idea if you want all the mess to be outside).
- To make it seem more "tent like," place an old tablecloth or blanket over the top of the table.
- Use colorful, unbreakable platters, bowls, and plates.
- Scatter unused gummy worms across the table.
- Serve the tea from a teapot and use china teacups if you aren't too afraid of breakage. It will make the kids feel special.
- You will be sure to get a laugh if you give your guests a plastic, bendable drinking straw to drink their tea. Give them permission to slurp away. Remember it is about breaking the rules and having fun.
- Scatter colorful balloons and boas on the floor under the table.
- If you can, crawl under the table and join the party. I guarantee you will create a lifelong memory!

Edible Flowers

www.sweetfields.com—candied flowers

www.localharvest.org—edible flowers
in your area

Baking Needs: Cookie Cutters, Stencils, and Baking Accessories

www.fancyflours.com

Tea

www.vintagetea.com

Great Tearooms in the South

www.teabiz.org

Southern Food Products

www.lowcountryproduce.com—pickled items
and sweet potato butter

www.blazerspecialtyfoods.com—awesome
pimento cheese

Ethnic Dinnerware, Glassware, and Accessories

www.worldmarket.com

Cooking and Tea Accessories, Table Linens, and Gadgets

www.anthropologie.com

www.cookswarehouse.com

www.crateandbarrel.com

www.potterybarn.com

www.surlatable.com

Party Supplies

www.worldmarket.com

www.partycity.com

www.plumparty.com

Sea Shells and Sea Accessories

www.seashellcity.com

Cacao Nibs and Chocolate

www.scharffenberger.com

www.ghirardelli.com

Bubble Tea Accessories

www.bobadirect.com

Acknowledgments

This book is a compilation of many wonderful people working together to help make my dream come true. Without the love and support of my husband, Joe, this book would not have become a reality. You are not only a great husband but have been my business advisor, financial supporter, editor, food tester, and taster of thousands of cups of tea. Thank you, Joe, for believing in my dream and embracing the fact that real men do drink tea!

My daughter, Kate, has been a great assistant to me, especially when it came to test kitchen cleanup and official taster. You have sacrificed your time to help me, and I couldn't have done it without your support and assistance!

My sister, Wendy Mcneece, has been fixing my verbiage since I was born. I do have a tendency to mix things up a bit. Thank you for fixing my mistakes and always knowing what I really meant to say.

Thank you to Yelena Shalansky for caring enough about your clients and their work to connect Lauren Rubinstein and me together for this project. Lauren, your pictures are beautiful, and you made my words come alive with your wonderful gift of photography. Thanks also to Annette Joseph, who understood my vision for this book and ran with it. Your styling is beautiful and exactly how I envisioned each party in mind.

A big thank you to Harvest House Publishers and Jean Christen for listening to my crazy ideas for a tea book and believing in the project. It has been a pleasure to work with everyone at Harvest House.

A special note of thanks to Emilie Barnes for writing from her heart about tea. *If Teacups Could Talk* was the first book I read on tea, and it began my dream of having a tea business someday. You have inspired many to drink and entertain with tea in a whole new way!